The Beauty and Biology of the Human Body

a Sexy Story

by

Larry A. Yff

TABLE of CONTENTS

2

I love my body and so does God! I mean, this thing is the real deal! He designed it so we can have excellent sex, scratch our backs, pick our nose, put our shoes on and cook, fry or bake chicken. Things no other life-form on planet Earth can do or thought about doing.

It's like we each have a hand-tailored, custom-fitted Earth space-suit. I say that because we can naturally breathe any air within the boundaries of Earth's protective Ozone Layer; yet we would literally die if we were to go past the Ozone without a space-helmet on. Everything about our bodies is designed for this one-of-a-kind, one-in-a-million planet.

Not even science with all its' nerds and brainpower can create humans...without using the sperm and egg from a male and a female human. For the record, and believe me they've been in secret labs for years trying to create human life without using humans, they have failed miserably every time. *No* robots or form of artificial intelligence can create a human.

We are a special species. We have access to the creativity and wisdom of God's laws and thoughts and can think on a level no other life form on this planet can come close to. There isn't a single animal that can use a power drill correctly AND drive a car AND count money correctly.

This book will shed light on the shortcomings of artificial intelligence and the amazing shit our bodies, fueled by human intelligence, are capable of and do every second of the day. You'll hopefully understand that God naturally did His thing with us so there's no need to mess with it. It's all good. Once you wrap your noodle around the message in this book, this is what should happen in your life:

1. You will start having the best sex ever

2. You will want to get married according to God's definition
    of marriage

3. You won't want to drink alcohol or do drugs

4. You will start using your Planet Fitness membership on a
    regular basis

5. If you're a man, you won't want to cut your dick off and
    get fake titties sewn on your chest to try and become
    something you can never be: a woman

6. You will save money because you won't want to go to
    Brazil now to get 10 pounds of butt-shaping plastic,
    cement, rubber, feathers, fat or whatever the fuck they
    inject in your ass anymore

Now, you have to remember I'm not a biologist or
whatever it is that studies the human body. I'm just a guy. I'm
just a guy with a body that has learned some amazing shit about
the human body that I want to share with you because this shit

changed my life, saved my life and improved my sex life. Need I

say more? Enough chit-chat, let's get into it...

CHAPTER ONE

<u>Head</u>

We're about to talk about the body and I think it's best we start at the top with the head and work our way down to the toes, okay? Cool.

It doesn't matter who your parents are or where you grew up or what kind of work you do or don't do. Us humans, all of us, are the real deal! We are all the shit! Our minds and bodies, controlled by our amazing brains, have no equal or competition on this planet. We are each wonderfully and uniquely made, one of a kind, custom-built individuals designed to manage our own little piece of this ball we call Earth.

I *really* love the brain. Can any artificially-programmed "thing" wake up, take a shit, take a shower, shave, take a bus to work, cuss out the boss, get fired, go to a local bar and get white-

7

boy wasted, wake up in a stranger's bed the next morning, take an Uber home, drink a detox smoothie and start searching the web for a new job all in 24 hours? I don't think so! A human with a human brain is the only life form that can pull all that off! Ha! In your face, artificial intelligence! Score "1" for human intelligence and "0" for artificial intelligence!

There is so much talk about how smart Artificial Intelligence (A.I.) is, but it's artificial. It's fake. Artificial does mean fake, right?!? I mean, really folks, it *literally* says "artificial" right in the name! It's like the packet that says "artificial sweetener". It's not a natural sweetener like sugar. It tastes like sugar. It sweetens your food like sugar…but it's' not sugar. It's a substitute. A fake. Something that's not real. An imitation.

I don't like fake shit…do you? Plus, our basic-ass brain operating on 10% of its potential is smarter than any Artificial Intelligence out there! Even my brain that has been through addictions to porn, coke and crack has more creative, powerful intelligence than any finely-tuned, artificial intelligence system on the planet.

I may be entering an area I'm not supposed to be talking about…but somebody has to. I mean, it's getting ridiculous! Somebody has to stop and tell the truth about our bodies and its designs. We're all basically Superman or Superwoman or Cat Woman or Aqua Man or Thor or any of those super-heroes you see in the movies except we don't have the script-writers, abs, capes and bodysuits!

Quick story: I saw a show where a guy had an accident when he was younger and had to get a fake eyeball. As he got older, he thought it would be cool to have a robotic eyeball like Arnold Schwarzenegger in the Terminator…so that's what he did! He believed an eyeball operating with artificial intelligence is better than a human eyeball.

Then there are the bio-hackers. These non-medically, un-certified, mentally unstable groups of individuals are cutting themselves open and putting all types of computer software and chips in their bodies! They are under the belief that the human body is imperfect and needs the help of artificial intelligence to improve it.

You know how you hear about how smart Artificial Intelligence is? Well, did you know your brain is smarter than any Fake Intelligence system out there? Seriously. The human brain has all kinds of shit going on that Fake Intelligence can't process or handle.

Let's start off with the basics of human development. The human body starts off as one big ass cell. It then starts to break apart and split into sections. This means your cells are multiplying, splitting and following some type of DNA code that allows different cells to form different parts of the body.

Any sperm cell that hooks up with any egg cell in any uterus is going to, on its own, transform. Somehow, these 2 cells have a natural code in them that allows them to start splitting, fusing, multiplying and splicing into billions of cells. Some of these cells form the legs, some form the eyes and on and on until you have a fully developed human. Here's something you may not have thought about...

Your drunk-ass dad walked into a bar. He saw the coked-up stripper who would eventually and officially become your mom, stripping on stage and he tipped her $1,000. He thought he was tipping her $10 in singles, but he was so drunk, well, he fucked up and instead of giving her 10 singles, he gave her ten $100 bills from his freshly cashed paycheck.

Your mom thought he was a rich drunk she could get some money out of, so she told him to meet her after her stage act for some "VIP time". He waited. They hooked up.

He didn't know her real name and she didn't want to know his. To him, she was "Cherry Bomb" and to her, he was just some nameless, rich sucker who walked up to the stage, told her he loved her and that he "wanted her to be the mother of his next child", stuffed her bikini bottoms with a wad of bills and sat down.

She thought he was the typical, strip-club, "I love you!!!!" patron, but in his own way, she also thought he was "disgustingly cute" and told him if his money was right...he could get a baby tonight! And here you are...

My point is, just in case you're wondering, even those 2 dumbasses can hook up and create the most powerful life form on the planet: a human! Take that in for a second! Even in our most drunkest, stupidest, unconscious state, we can *still* do something the most sophisticated artificial intelligence-programmed "thing" could and can never do!

Our sperm and egg cells are able to produce another powerful human being regardless of the human pair's skin color, hair type, education, language, economic class or any other human trait we use to categorize, divide and classify ourselves. So, check this out...

It takes about 6 weeks for the cells in the human fetus to split off and start forming the brain. The brain has 4 major sections and oh, I have another Terminator movie reference.

The 4 parts of the brain begin to come together like that terminator in the movie Terminator Two. Remember the part where the new model terminator is wearing that cop uniform and the old terminator cuts him in half? Here's how that went...

New Terminator was chasing Old Terminator. Old Terminator took a sword or something metal and cut New Terminator right through his head down to the middle of his chest. New Terminator didn't die.

New Terminator started chasing Old Terminator even though the top half of his body was split in half. As he was running, his body began to "zip" itself back together and form one solid, physical shape again.

Our brain is like that. Without any type of outside instruction, certain cells just start forming into brain cells. These cells form the sections of the brain and somehow, they all start to fuse together and there you have it! You've now got a fully functioning, 4-part brain!

Are you amazed? Can you tell me any Artificial Intelligence system that can start off as a cell and begin to divide itself and, without somebody on the outside giving it some type of computer code, start transforming into a brain, a heart, lungs, veins, legs, arms, etc.? Let me stay focused on the brain...

This thing looks like a blob of oatmeal-colored sausage links but is incredibly powerful! There are like 80 billion neurons in there! That means there are sparks of energy sparking all day long whether you are awake, asleep, passed-out drunk or playing soccer. Think about this...

When you wake up, did you know your brain has been doing all kinds of calculations and algorithms the entire time? Yup. It has been receiving signals from your entire body.

The brain is helping you block out your neighbor's loud-ass, barking-ass, yelping-ass dog so you can get some shut-eye. While it was doing that, it was also controlling the muscles in your eyelids so your eyes stay shut.

While it's doing that, it's keeping track of your bladder and controlling those muscles so you don't piss on yourself.

While it's doing that, it's monitoring your body temperature and if you're getting too cold, it's sending signals to the muscles in your arms and hands to move so they can pull the blanket up and over your body.

In the event you are too hot, your brain is telling your sweat cells to release sweat to cool your ass down and if that doesn't do the trick, your brain is tapping into your memory bank so you can remember where the thermostat is so you can go turn the air conditioning on while you're half asleep without tripping over shit and falling down the stairs.

While it's doing that, your brain is also acting like a movie producer because it's playing dreams in your head on the big screen. Who did you think was behind the scenes of the fantasy-dream you enjoyed last night?

It was your brain doing all the work while you were sleeping with that big, cheesy-ass grin on your face. Your brain was taking care of all the casting call and prop needs to make sure everything was perfect for you to have the perfect date night in your dreams.

It was your brain that made sure your "dream girl" looked exactly like the stripper-girl you fantasized about earlier.

It was your brain that made sure your "dream strip-club" looked identical to the local strip-club you were at earlier.

It was your brain who made sure your "dream girl" looked exactly like the real-life, stripper-chick from the exact size and shape of her full, beautiful lips down to the exact size and color of her 4-inch, red-bottom stilettos. Our brain is amazing when it comes to remembering details, isn't it?!?

While it's doing that, let's not forget about your heart. You have to have a beating heart to remain alive. Who controls that? You guessed it...the brain!

The brain is making sure some veins are sending blood to your heart and making sure the other veins, known as arteries, are taking blood away from your heart. It has to monitor this so your heart performs this complete cycle at least once every second.

Let's not forget about your lungs. Those things have to take in and let out air every second as well so you can stay alive. The brain is in charge of monitoring all of that activity as well. If you happen to be in a deep sleep, the brain is in charge of letting you know there is a build-up of fluid and it's time for you to cough and get that shit out of your system. Let's get back to the blood for a second...

There are billions of blood cells being pushed through your body and through every organ and inch of tissue that makes you who you are. The brain monitors any type of blockage that occurs and sends signals to other cells to correct it.

The blood in your stomach breaks down food. The brain is responsible for making sure the stomach has the right mix of blood and hydrochloric acid in it so you don't get the bubble guts. Speaking of bubble guts...

While you're still asleep, your brain is making sure your O-ring is doing what it's supposed to be doing. For you technical people, the O-ring is in your ass. It's not really an O-ring. It's actually a circular muscle that makes sure you don't shit on yourself while you're off in la-la land enjoying your dreams.

What we just went over is only about half the functions our brain does while we sleep. If we were to get into all the functions it did while we were awake it would be fucking bonkers...so, let's do it!

When you wake up feeling well-rested, remember your brain hasn't slept a wink. Your brain doesn't rest until your dead. That blob of mushy stuff literally is on the job 24 hours a day, 7 days a week. Do you know how exhausting that would be?

By the time you're 10 years old, your poor brain has been working for around 350,000 days straight with no time off! Getting back to you waking up...

Alright, now you're awake. The brain now has to bring the memories to the front of your thoughts that help you remember whose house you're in, where the bathroom, toilet, sink, toothbrush and other shit is so you can clean yourself up and start the day.

While it's coordinating all of these functions, it's still doing all of the functions we talked about it doing while you were sleeping. That means, when you wake up, you have just given your brain a bazillion more things to do on top of the gazillion things it was doing while you were asleep.

Your brain is still monitoring and regulating your body temp, blood pressure, digestive activity, breathing and heartbeat…and now it has to take in and process all of the data your open eyeballs and ears are taking in!

The crazy thing is that each day, the brain is processing new shit and storing all of this data in your memory. Each day, there is something new your eyes, ears, nose and mouth are taking in and each day, there is something new your hands are coming in contact with.

That stock report you're reading on your desk isn't the same one you read yesterday. That means your brain has already stored the important elements of yesterday's stock-market, gambling stats and now it has to replace some of them, update some of them and add new ones to the memory banks.

We've started with the head and haven't even gotten past the damn brain! Oh yeah, science tells us our brain can process around 10 billion bits of information…every second! I have no ideal what a bit is, but I know that's a whole lot of shit our brain is processing! Let's switch gears and talk about Fake, I mean, Artificial Intelligence...

Artificial Intelligence is based on processing information as well. These programs can process millions and maybe billions of bits of information a second as well, but here's the difference:

Artificial Intelligence can only do what it's processed to do. If there is AI being used in the military, for instance, that thing can only do a limited number of functions. A radar can be programmed to take in data from 1,000 different sources and then take action 100 different ways...but that's all it can do.

The human body is using its intelligence to monitor a human's physical surrounding while accessing the spiritual and mental realms. A sonar radar, for instance, can't monitor all the shit it's supposed to be monitoring and feel loved or fall in love with another radar...it can only monitor 1,000 different sources and then take action 100 different ways. That's all it can do.

The same can be said for any piece of high-tech, Artificial Intelligence weaponry. Yes, there are missile's that can be fired from California that can hit little Danny's toy car sitting in his front yard somewhere in Delaware...but that's all it can do.

That missile can't take a detour and then circle back towards its' intended target. Artificial intelligence objects and machinery can only do what they are programmed to do without exception. If there is an exception, it has to be programmed or coded into its' system. Let's move on to the eyeballs...

Our eyeballs are designed to take in everything that is going on and sending all of that data to the brain for processing...as if the brain doesn't already have its' hands full!

From the moment we wake up and open our eyes, we are scanning. We are scanning what's in front of and with our peripheral vision, we are also scanning shit that's happening to the left, right, top and bottom of our forward line of view.

Some people say the eyes are the windows to the soul. I think they're right. There is something about the design of our eyeballs that allow us to look at someone and somehow tell if they're bullshitting us or not. People who look at us can also tell if we are hurt, happy or in love just by looking at an apparently lifeless thing we call an eyeball.

The placement of our eyes is perfect. They are positioned so we can focus primarily on what's going on in front of us, which is the most important area we should be looking at. It's also attractive with our eyes right there. It makes for the perfect design.

What if our eyes were positioned on the top half of our head instead of in the middle, like lions? Lions have their eyes higher up on their heads so when they are hunting, they can stay low to the ground, hidden and still see their intended targets.

Would you be attracted to a person with eyeballs on the side of their head like a chameleon? Probably not. That is *not* attractive or functionable for humans. Speaking about attraction, people get surgeries to have their eyeballs appear to be rounder or more slanted or wear color contacts because they don't like the natural color of their eyes.

Personal note: When I was younger, I wanted to be "white and attractive" so I hated my brown eye color. I wanted them to be more of a royal blue color like my big brother and all the white males at my church and school had. I even considered getting colored contacts at one point to make my eyes any color but brown.

Our eyelashes are designed to help keep dust and debris out of our eyes. We naturally come with eye-protectors! Our eyebrows are designed to divert water and sweat from dripping down our foreheads and into our eyes. This means we naturally have another layer of eye-protection built into our faces!

Everything about our natural design, down to the smallest detail, has a natural purpose, but we tend to get it mixed up. Since eyes are such a beautiful, centered, focal point of our faces, a lot of people have been brainwashed to believe the best way to highlight this natural beauty is to spend billions of dollars a year getting fake eyelashes!

They get fake eyelashes glued on and the glue permanently messes up the skin around their eyelids. This fake process has also been known to make your real eyelashes with real functions fall out! Why? The purpose, design and size of our natural eyelashes is to protect us, but when we glue 3-inch eyelashes on, they now have no real purpose other than to make the person with them look unnatural.

The nose. The nose is also right in the center of the face and like the eyeballs, it is constantly sending data to the brain for processing. In the event we use our nose to sniff food, the nose sends smells to the brain to process and let us know if the food we are smelling is good, mildewed and what flavor it is.

The nose has a bunch of wet shit in it called mucus, I think. Anyways, this fluid helps prevent lots of viruses, dust and dirt from entering our system as well. Anything entering our body through our nose has a direct effect on our brain.

I took advantage of this function and used my nose for decades to sniff cocaine. I enjoyed misusing my nose to get the most direct high possible. I was burning nose hairs, directly fucking my brain up and preventing my nose from serving the natural functions it was designed for, but I'm not the only one guilty of not knowing what a nose is for…

Some people believe the nose has to be a certain size or shape in order to be beautiful so they get surgeries. This process takes away from the nose's natural function. See? We humans have a tendency to take a good thing and try and change it for

what we believe are beautifying purposes.

Our nose has a natural function and naturally has hairs in it

that we love to cut out. We cut them out for looks. Everything

we tend to do to our faces and bodies, in our eyes, tends to be to

fulfill our picture of what we think beauty is...fuck function!

Personal note: When I was younger, I wanted to be "white

and attractive" so I hated my nose. My nose is a mix between

Michael Jackson's original nose and the original nose of one of his

big brothers. I would take pictures with my head facing down so

you couldn't see the actual size of my nose...or so I thought. The

white males at my church and school all had long, skinny noses

and I wanted to look more like them.

Our mouths are also part of the center design of our

heads/faces. What if our mouth was located on top of our noses?

If that was the case, our nose would have no function and that means we wouldn't be able to sniff things or breath through our nose properly.

It wouldn't work because the food we are eating would fall from our mouths into our nasal cavity. See? Intentional design is everywhere in and on our bodies.

The mouth is designed to chew and breakdown food. It has some wet shit in it that has acid. This acid helps keep our teeth clean as well as break down food particles left in our mouths. Without a mouth, we wouldn't be able to naturally get food into our systems and without food, well, we'd die.

As is the case with every other body part, the mouth is constantly sending feedback to the brain letting us know the candy we ate is too sweet or too sour and the brain takes in that data so we can remember to avoid that particular candy purchase later on in life.

Personal note: When I was younger, I wanted to be "white and attractive" and hated my mouth. I didn't see any of the other white males at my church or school with lips like mine. While none of the white boys at my high-school had beards and/or mustaches, I noticed the black boys at the other high schools did and I wanted one...but I didn't dare because I tried one time and one of my white friends made fun of me and I wanted to fit in with them, so I never had a mustache or beard during my high school years.

Out tongue is said to be the strongest, pound-for-pound muscle in our body. It's designed to move food around in our mouths and has taste buds to help us decipher different flavors and tastes. It is the perfect size and design to move food around as well as help get food out from between our teeth and without a tongue, we wouldn't be able to talk or make certain sounds.

Our mouth is lined with lips. The lips and tongue work together to help us talk. These lips have a natural function. They are designed to allow us to chew food without the broken-down food falling out of our mouths. They are also used to help babies suck on bottles or nipples. Without them, babies couldn't get any nutrients. Pretty essential, huh?

But once again, as we humans typically do, we mistake and misuse our lips. We get injections in them to make them bigger and more kissable looking. 9 out of 10 times though, it makes the person's lips and entire face look unnatural and fake. Often times there are also lifelong problems from these injections. Are they worth it? Is it worth tampering with the natural design and form of our lips for "beauty" purposes?

Last but not least is our ears. Our ears are designed on either side of our heads. This covers all of our bases: our eyes help us see what's in front of us and our ears help us process what's going on around us from both sides. There's really not a lot to say about ears, but I know some nosey ass people who would hate to be without them.

Actually, after I said that, I googled ears to see what else they do and I found out they somehow help us keep ourselves balanced! That's important. They are pretty technical on the inside and like the nose and eyes, the ears have natural protection in the form of wax. Wax naturally builds up in the ears to protect outside elements from having direct access to our brains.

That's about it for our heads, but I just wanted you to see how much planning and design goes into every body part. No body part is in the wrong place or has no function and that's amazing! Let's head down to the torso...

CHAPTER TWO

<u>Torso</u>

Like I said earlier, everything about our body is amazing. We talked about the head and now we are moving on to our amazing torso.

Some of the other body parts such as the eyes, ears and nose have a natural protective element to them in the form of physical shape, mucus and hair. The brain has a natural protective shield of hard bone called a skull. The other essential organs in our body, specifically the torso, also have a natural protective layer.

Our heart, lungs, kidneys and liver are all housed within the human body's protective bone casing we call the rib cage. The rib cage is a bunch of, well, rib bones that wrap around our bodies from the spinal cord to the front of our body and meet in a bone called our chest plate. I think I want to start with the heart

1st because we already went into it a little bit earlier so it will be

short...

The heart is our organ where all the blood that goes to any

part of our body flows in and out. This may seem like nothing

significant, but think about this: every second, your heart takes in

blood and pumps out blood from over 60,000 miles of veins and

arteries! If yo' ass ain't amazed by that figure...yo' ass ain't got a

heart or a brain!

Did you read what I just wrote? 60,000 miles of veins and

arteries are running through each and every one of our bodies

and is being shuttled, pumped and pulled back and forth through

our entire body at least once every second! Can you tell me any

type of artificial intelligence supported machinery that can do

that?

Personal note: I had addictions to blow and crack for years. I was aware, but not how significantly, I was fucking my heart up. The cocaine would get into my bloodstream and every time my heart beat, it would pump those chemicals through my entire body. Do you know where the blood goes that gets pumped through your body? Everywhere. With every beat of your heart, whatever you have in your bloodstream gets pumped through your heart, brain, liver, kidney, etc. I was steadily fucking up my finely-tuned system with drugs and I'm sure I have some type of avoidable, leftover damage from that activity.

If you can, then I want you to find me a piece of machinery that can not only do that, but one that also has the power to fix itself. Yeah, when there is a puncture in one of the arteries or veins, the brain finds out about it and tells the blood to start stopping the leak by clotting itself!

I did plumbing work and I dealt with leaks a lot. I hated dealing with them because they were so messy. What would typically happen is a copper pipe might bust and water would start shooting all over the place. I would have to turn off the water to that pipe so I could fix it. Sometimes, this required me to turn off all the water to the whole house so I could stop the leak.

Here's what's amazing about our bodies and the heart: when there is a "leak" in a blood vessel, the heart continues to pump blood through the whole body every second *while* sending blood-clotting agents to the hole to fix it without missing a beat!

Just like working with copper pipes though, if the leak is too bad, the blood vessels may need to be replaced if they can't be repaired. *Unlike* working with copper pipes, if the leak can't be fixed, the result is the person with the "leak" can bleed out and die. Well, I guess there is a similarity in that the leak from a copper pipe could be so bad that the entire house could flood and have to be demolished. Moving on…

While the brain is monitoring all movement of all blood cells in all the 60,000 miles of veins and arteries, it also has to monitor the lungs. We are born with 2 lungs, which is pretty cool because we can technically live with just one. It's like our body came equipped with a spare "tire", but it's a spare lung instead.

The lungs provide air so we can talk and smell. They also are able to process any air that comes into the body to instantly make it match our body temperature. Delivering oxygen to all the cells in your body is another necessary function of the lungs, but we're not done…

The lungs also process and remove any waste gases you may have breathed in, including carbon dioxide, through our exhaling process. those are some pretty important functions and that incredible brain of yours, yes, it's monitoring and correcting all of that activity as well.

Lungs that are full of smoke can't operate properly because they weren't made to inhale and process smoke in a healthy way. Millions of people have died from cancer in their lungs as a result of smoking cigarettes. I'm not about to get into a debate about weed-smoke, but just know our body has no natural need for smoke and smoke in any form isn't healthy for us.

Personal note: I used to have an addiction to crack cocaine. I would inhale a big hit of crack smoke and get a sexual rush through my body. After years of doing this, I'm sure I have some type of avoidable damage to my lungs that I can't measure.

We also have a vital organ called the liver. This muscle is responsible for doing a lot of processing. Any blood that passes through our stomachs or intestines also passes through the liver. The liver is responsible to pull and store certain nutrients from that blood and store them. It also acts as a natural filter. Let's talk about filters really quick...

Cars have filters. Furnaces have filters. Everything that "breathes" has some sort of necessary filtration system in it and, since we have lungs and are able to breath, our body naturally has a filtration system built in to it! It naturally goes above and beyond and provides us with a *dual,* filtration system!

The lungs are used to filter the air and the liver is used to filter liquids and this is where we misuse the function of this filter and bring unavoidable pain and diseases into our bodies. The liver typically gets messed up from a fluid we commonly intake called alcohol.

Every shot we take, every beer we guzzle and every glass of wine we sip passes through the liver. The liver is trying to store nutrients for the body and process necessary liquids like blood, but we humans are constantly making its' job harder by having it process alcohol on top of its' other responsibilities. Too much alcohol consumption and we can die or at least destroy our livers by drinking alcohol.

I have a friend who drank every day. He *had* to drink every

day. His body became physically dependent on that fluid called

alcohol, just like it was dependent on the fluid we call blood. Both

were essential for him to stay alive. He went to jail one time and

almost died because his body wasn't able to have any alcohol.

The liver is so important that you can die if you don't have

it. You can live with part of a liver, but that can be a hard life

because your body isn't able to function properly or process

digestive blood like it's supposed to. Since the liver detoxes the

body, without it, or with a small part of your liver, you will die

pretty fast.

There are chemicals that will begin to build up in your

body and since your liver isn't processing them and flushing them

out your system through our piss, our body will basically become

a toxic waste-dump and we would die.

Alright, I think we have to slow down and do a quick re-cap of our body:

1. Our bodies are custom-built for Earth

2. Our bodies have vital, built-in filtration systems

3. Our bodies have essential, built-in protective framing and structure

4. Our bodies have a brain that controls any and all physical *and* spiritual functions we are involved in and processes millions of bits of data and information a minute

5. Our human intelligence is far smarter than any artificial intelligence system we have created

Amazing, right?!? Everything about our bodies is made for us to enjoy this journey on planet Earth and everything on and in planet Earth is designed to work naturally and seamlessly with our bodies.

I'm not using this book to preach to you about God or biology, but I do want you to start appreciating the unique design our bodies have. Maybe, after looking at all the systems and functions we are all capable of, we can stop destroying our bodies with certain activities.

The brain. I told you in the introduction or the 1st chapter that I love the brain. I say that now, but when I was in the midst of my addictions, I didn't give a fuck about a brain. I didn't give a fuck about a brain, a lung, a heart, a kidney...nothing! All I cared about was getting high to fulfill some personal fantasy or to "help" me get through the day.

There are so many diseases and situations that are easily avoidable that *we* put our bodies through. We fall victim to the messages we are constantly being flooded by from the media that it's cool to "party" and get drunk. Mainstream commercials and movies that get the most exposure and highest rankings push drinking sex as being recreational and good for us.

Let's not talk about popular songs. The majority of them are telling us it's cool to take shots of alcohol or pop pills. I'm just as guilty for being swayed by them. When I would get restless or angry, I would love to blast Tupac. It gave me peace in that mood.

When I would go to the strip-clubs, the music with lyrics that talked about some chick shakin' her ass or some group of dudes having fun "fuckin' all these bitches and all these hoes" or a song blasting "don't stop, pop that ass...now bend over and touch your toes" or some sex-pill-popping lyrics made me feel comfortable, relaxed and hyped-up in that environment.

I'm only talking about this because I like to be honest. I pretty much was fucking up all my organs, without exception, just trying to make my own rules. When I was under the impression that I was in control of my own body, I was able to do that, but once I had to stop and take a look at my body, and everything around me, I had to say, "Somebody intentionally designed all this shit! There is too much natural law and order for there not to be a designer/creator behind the scenes of all this technical, creative design I see in nature and in my own body. It would be in my best interest to contact this designer/creator to see what laws I should be following to be able to fully appreciate life here on Earth."

After reviewing historical records, checking out scientific data and reading several eyewitness accounts regarding the creation of the universe and some spiritual testimonies, I chose God. I chose God as being that designer/creator and I never looked back. From that point on I began to appreciate my brain and the importance of waking up with a clear head. Not just to live a healthy life, but to be able to operate at my highest physical and spiritual level...

Wait a minute! I was talking about the body and I went off track! I'm sorry! I can't help it! If you see something incredible, it's hard not to share it so, when I see all the crazy, technical, natural design in our bodies and since I believe God is responsible for it, I start thinking about how smart He is and how...

Nope. I'm not gonna preach right here. If you wanna go down that path, you need to get my book called, "I can't 'Just Say No!': a non-Reagan Recovery Story" or "The Power is in The Plan". Let's get back to talking about the body, more specifically the torso and the vital organs in it…

While all of our vital organs in the torso are protected by the ribcage, a couple of them aren't totally protected and with good reason. The stomach and intestines aren't confined by the ribcage and that allows us to eat and expand our stomachs without putting a lot of pressure from the inside on our ribcage. Our stomach is another fascinating aspect of our bodies that is perfect in its' natural design and yes, us humans found a way to fuck that up as well…

Everything we eat or drink goes down our throat and into the stomach. Everything. This means the stomach has to be designed to process any and every type of food or drink we could ever possibly take in.

In the event that we take in something harmful for our bodies, the stomach is designed to make us throw up and get it out of our systems. The food and drink that is good for us gets processed and broken down with our blood and stomach acid.

It's an incredible design that allows us to have extremely strong acid in our stomachs without it being housed in a glass bottle or jar. Our stomach acid, hydrochloric acid, is as strong as car battery acid and can dissolve metal; yet our stomach can house it and use it to break down food so we can have energy, fight sickness and grow.

Here's a crazy fact: if your skin or eyes comes in contact with hydrochloric acid, serious injury can occur and you also need to be very careful how you store it...but this acid within our bodies is healthy and is somehow stored properly within our stomachs!

Remember I said we humans tend to fuck up things that are natural? Well, when people want to get healthy and in shape, instead of working out, eating less, drinking more water or getting more sleep, some of us would rather have a surgery that cuts our bodies open so our stomach size can be reduced.

The thinking is if we have a smaller stomach, we won't be able to hold as much food so we won't want to eat as much. I would potentially believe in this process if the surgery reduced the size of the stomach AND somehow was able to chemically change our thinking process into not wanting to eat as much.

Thinking "if you can't eat a lot, you can't gain weight" opens you up to weight-loss failure. Losing weight is more about mentally controlling how much you take in and how much energy you expand throughout the day. Surgeries like that are temporary fixes that tend to hurt the body because they go against the natural processes of the body.

There are millions of people who got these surgeries that 1) regret it and 2) gained the majority of the weight they "lost" within a short period of time. Let's talk about body-altering

surgeries for a minute...

I don't understand how licensed doctors are able to keep

their licenses performing these and other types of surgeries.

Getting plastic surgery has been proven to have so many

detrimental effects on our bodies it's ridiculous!

People are dying from getting stuff injected in their ass

cheeks. People faces are looking like mummies from getting

multiple facial surgeries. People are also having serious health

complications when they get their titties bigger or lip injections to

have sexxxy, full lips.

99.9% of these surgeries are for personal cosmetic reasons

and I think it's a shame the medical profession is allowing licensed

members of that profession to perform the non-emergency, non-

essential surgeries they are performing every day, raking in

billions of dollars in revenue without caring about the patient's mental or physical health. There are always exceptions, but that's

my view…

After food goes through the stomach, our body has a built-

in garbage-disposal system. This process is carried out with our

intestines. We have a large and a small intestine. These long,

folded tubes are responsible for continuing the food breakdown

process the stomach started and allows the nutrients and water

to enter the rest of our body.

Anything that can't be processed or is unneeded in our

bodies will eventually make its way from the stomach, through

the large intestine, the small intestine and out our bodies in the

form of solid waste AKA shit/poop or liquid waste AKA piss/urine.

Before we move to the other parts of our bodies, I want to

say that I find it absolutely amazing how our body's internal

organs are able to do all these multiple functions naturally. It's

amazing because when we build high-tech factories, machinery and cars we make sure all the functions our bodies have are in these things. Think about it…

Factories have to process waste from production…our bodies have a digestive/waste system that does this.

Factories and cars have to process the air through filters and exhaust systems…our bodies have lungs that do this.

Factories have to take in raw materials in order to produce a useful product…our bodies have a mouth that takes in raw materials for our bodies to process to keep us functioning in productive, useful ways.

That's all for the main part of the torso. Now let's get into the limbs that are attached to the torso…

CHAPTER THREE

Limbs

By limbs, I'm talking arms with the hands and legs with the feet. I'm breaking down that description because even though a limb is technically the arm and includes the hands, I think it's important to separate the 2 parts of the limbs and look at them individually. Legs first...

Our legs are designed to hold our body weight. They hold our body weight and allow us to walk forward or backward or jump upwards. It may seem like a simple design, but scientists and artificial intelligence workers are spending millions of man hours trying to make robots that can walk and jump as smoothly and naturally as humans do from an early age.

I've seen lots of robots and artificial intelligence "beings" walk and it looks horrible! It's like they put the mechanical legs of a spider onto human-style, robotic frames and it's some of the most ugly, awkward shit I've seen in all my life.

They are even trying to duplicate the natural walk of animals with artificial intelligence to make "horses" that can carry stuff. The "horses" are all able to carry stuff, but they all walk like they have something stuck in the buts and have horseshoes that are 3 sizes too small. The next time you're under the impression your legs are nothing special, google "images for walking robots" and tell me what you think...

The design of the knees makes it so we can stand straight up. They are designed to bend in only one direction. If they went both ways, humans wouldn't be able to do that simple act of standing still.

The legs are made of muscles, tendons and ligaments that are all attached to an internal frame called our bone structure. The leg bones are all linked to the rest of the entire human bone frame. The leg muscles are a very complex system with a built-in lubrication system. By that, I mean blood flows into the muscles to keep them flexible and strong; while the knees and other joints have another natural type of liquid lubricant that keeps them from grinding bone-on-bone.

This same design is seen in the automobile. Cars have things called tie-rods and wheel-bearings. The tie-rods help steer the car and rely on the wheel bearings similar to the arm or leg relying on the elbows and the knee. There are so many designs in our industrial and artificial intelligence that are built upon and similar to our human body that it makes our bodies even more amazing!

The legs are attached to the feet. Any of you thinking the feet aren't important have never stubbed your toe or had "athlete's foot" or something they call "corns" or "bunions" on your feet. The design of the leg and foot are so precise, any injury or change in the condition of the feet will affect the legs and the entire body.

Everything about our bodies is connected. If you get a "Charlie horse" in your leg, you won't be able to walk properly or stand up straight. You will also feel pain through your whole body because it has to adjust to the "Charlie horse". The same can be said for any injury or change in body structure because the body is designed to naturally work smoothly together, any flaw or hiccup in that natural system changes everything. I know we're talking about the limbs, but let's go off on another bunny trail and hop to another subject...

Our bodies are designed to function based on how our brain operates. If you tamper with the brain's ability to function, you affect the entire body. Alcohol is a substance that alters the way the brain functions. Anybody familiar with "beer goggles"? That's a term used to describe the event where somebody gets drunk and has sex with some body they wouldn't have had sex with if they weren't under the influence of alcohol. When you're

under the influence of alcohol, you see things *differently*.

For me, it was cocaine. If you met me while sober, you

would think I was one way, but if you came across me high, you

would see me as somebody completely differently. Once any

form of cocaine would enter my system, I would immediately

think sex, strip-clubs and porn.

Once I started getting high, there was no way to change

my brain out of this mode until I was forced to from an outside

element. Once high, my brain wouldn't be able to rationalize like

it normally would. I would get high and keep the family vehicle

overnight even though my wife would need it to take the kids to

school. My brain was under the influence of drugs and kept me

from functioning like a rational human being.

I'm giving you that as an example, because for a couple of

reasons. One reason is that I don't like to preach to people without letting them know what tripped me up and how I was able to recover, putting me in the position to preach, teach and help others.

The other reason is I want you to think about some situations you have been in and how it was *you,* nobody else, who got you in that predicament. Do you have lung cancer from smoking cigarettes? Is it the fault of the cigarette company? Did they make you smoke their product?

Are you in jail on a DUI? If so, whose fault is it? Is it the alcohol companies' fault? Were their strategic and intentional marketing and advertising campaigns so compelling and sexxxy that you thought drinking would make women like you more and make you look cool, so you started drinking and now have an alcohol problem?

I have to look at myself and ask myself the same questions. I lost about 4 teeth because my mouth wasn't healthy from years of drug abuse. Whose fault was it? Was it the guy who sold me the drugs? Did he make me smoke crack? Was it his fault for not trying to help me through my addiction?

I have found that 99% of my health problems were the direct results of my actions and decisions. Change your decision-making process and you can usually change your health, physical, mental and spiritual. Let me take a moment to talk about God...again...

We have a natural design in our bodies that, if we take care of our physical and mental health properly, we can function on the highest human level we possibly can. Here's where it gets tricky...

If we think we are somehow responsible for our own intricate and structurally-sound design, then we can try and achieve success in life by creating our own laws, guidelines and standards to reach this goal. There are many situations in life that fluctuate and change the rules and laws of the game of life. All laws change except for the laws God passed down for thousands of years for humans to follow.

In my experience, whenever I followed God's laws for personal, physical, business or any other type of success...I achieved it. When I left my ability to achieve up to one political party or another, or based on what one cultural group or another believes in, I found myself constantly chasing but never achieving.

God designed our bodies in such a way that we can achieve spiritual greatness by having a clear, functioning brain that is receptive to hearing from Him.

We can achieve physical greatness by eating the fruits and vegetables he gave us and getting rest, drinking lots of water and not drinking alcohol or putting drugs into our systems.

Do you see what I'm getting at? Success in life is predictable. All you have to do is follow God's laws for business, good health, sex and every other area of life and you can get it! I'm telling you this because, as I switched from following my own path to being accountable to God for all my ability and design, I began to find success in all areas of my life. Just sharing from a point of caring…

Shit! I went off track…again!!! I know some of my books can be hard to follow, but it's hard for me to stay on track. As I'm writing about one subject, it reminds me of God's influence in another subject and they all tie together so nicely that I seamlessly switch topics. This opens the door for me to share helpful information, but at a cost: my book goes from talking about limbs, eyeballs and fake asses to how God has changed my life and there I went off track again LOL!!!

Alright, let's talk about our arms and hands. Our arms are firmly attached to our mainframe torso with bones, muscles and tendons, but that's not all. Our arms are designed to be long enough to reach every area of our body. Why? Well, it's our hands that are attached to our arms that are used to comb our hair, put on our shoes and scratch our backs.

This means our arms need to move at certain angles to achieve all these tasks and yes, that design is naturally in our arms. Our arms come in 2 sections separated by elbows. The elbows for our arms are like the knees for our legs.

Our arms, just like our legs, have groups of muscles that are designed to push, pull, extend or contract depending on what function we are attempting to do. There is something interesting about the arms and hands that has me confused sometimes: left hand or right hand.

People are either right-handed or left-handed. If you're right-handed, you do everything with your right hand taking the lead and vice versa. I brush my teeth and write with my right hand, but when I try and do that activity with my left hand, I can't.

Actually, the same can be said about our feet. We are inclined to lead and use one over the other.

I have a tip for you: if you're right-handed, try switching and using your left. It's an excellent exercise for the brain, plus it will show you how the brain can adapt and adjust if you force it to. We all have the ability to change, redirect or correct the way we think and that changes the way we act.

When I use my left hand to brush my teeth, for instance, my brain is forced to create new thought patterns to allow the use of my left hand to do a function that the brain was used to telling the right hand to do. Changing your view changes your world, expands your ability, increases your knowledge base and ultimately determines whether or not you will be successful in life.

In nature, every animal species has "arms" and "hands" that fit its' purpose. Deer's have hooves, to they aren't built to hunt; meanwhile, lions and leopards have paws with retractable claws as "hands" and they are built for catching and killing prey animals. Humans also have hands that fit their function.

I already told you human arms are designed for us to be able to stretch and reach every part of our body, but it's the hands that determine what functions we can and cannot do. Our hands have 5 fingers and that is, as you already know I'm about to say, the perfect design to do what we were designed to do.

Now, I believe God created us and, according to the book in the Bible called Genesis, told us to "...have kids, manage and subdue the Earth and rule over all the animals and use the seed-bearing trees for food..." If you want to know more about this particular set of instructions God gave humans, check out my book, "Get a job, get laid, get a dog and recycle – God". For now, I'm just going to talk about the uses of the hands as it relates to fulfilling these tasks and not so much the principles behind it...

We are supposed to have sex. All animals and insects have sex to reproduce. Since I will be talking about our baby-making parts in the next section, let me just say having sex would be pretty hard if you didn't have hands.

We need to eat. Humans are the only species that has the ability to cook, boil, fry, season and bake food. In order to do this, we need hands. We need hands to hold spices, pluck chickens, peel oranges and cut steaks. If you don't believe me, try doing something simple like eating cereal with a spoon and not having a thumb. No other species of life on this planet has that capability and that's why they don't get to eat Lucky Charms, Captain Crunch or Golden Graham cereal out of bowls using a spoon without spilling shit all over the place.

I said we have 5 fingers. Each finger is designed to do different things. When you have all 5 functioning normally and in good health, every task you know how to do is easily done. Just like with other body parts, if any part of the hand is hurt or broken, the easiest of jobs won't get done or they will get done

with a lot of discomfort and clumsiness.

Let's stick with the cooking example. Open the cabinet,

reach up and grab some Lawry's seasoning salt, take the top off

and pour some out onto a piece of fresh chicken. Now do that

same task without your thumb. If that's still easy, try and do it

without any one of your fingers and I'll bet it becomes such a hard

task, you might break out in a sweat or never get a crumb of

Lawry's seasoning anywhere near your piece of chicken.

I was in an accident and I crushed all the bones in my left

wrist. I couldn't sleep because I couldn't roll over on that arm

while it was in a cast. I couldn't go to the bathroom well, because

it was hard for me to grab the toilet paper roll and tear enough a

couple of squares off to wipe my ass. I couldn't hold a sandwich

or cut my own steak up. Now, some of these things I learned to

do after a while, but my point is, our fingers have the best design to allow us to eat like we're supposed to at the top of the food chain.

We are also supposed to rule over the animals of the Earth. If we had hooves, we wouldn't be able to catch all the animals we currently catch or be able to walk them on leashes or perform life-saving surgeries. If we had claws, the same would be true for that. Even if we had 4 fingers and no thumb, for instance, we wouldn't be able to properly do everything we do right now in our role of dominating and controlling all animal life.

Try and walk your dog without your middle fingers or your thumbs. There are a million examples I could give you that get my point across about the importance to detail God had when He 1) made our hands and 2) told us to subdue all plant and animal life on this planet. Speaking of controlling plant life…

We are the only species on this planet that can farm. No other species of life comes close to farming anything. I guess monkeys would come the closest because they also have hands similar to us with 4 fingers and a thumb. Because of this, they can reach up and grab fruit off of trees and pry or peel them open and that's the closest example in nature I can give you.

If you've ever used a plow, picked cotton or watered plants in a pot, you will attest to the fact that having all 5 fingers the way we have them is perfect and there's no need to go down the path of giving you a bunch of examples like how hard it would be to plant a seed if you didn't have thumbs.

I said monkeys are the closest animal to be able to perform some of the functions we do with our hands. Monkeys can hold a hammer. They can also hold a drill or a baseball bat. Even with this most basic closeness to humans, they lack the brainpower to understand how the game of baseball is played, how to hammer nails or screw drywall screws while hanging drywall.

Alright, there you have it for limbs. Some chapters are smaller than others because making some points doesn't require as much time as others. Understanding our hands are the perfect design doesn't take a whole lot of effort to see or comprehend...

CHAPTER FOUR

Private Parts

As always, I like to let you know ahead of time that a lot of my books share the same topics. In this case, the book "The Purpose of a Penis: Nature Stories" does a good job of going into more details about our private parts. The focal point of *this* book sticks with the basic design and purpose of our natural, God-designed bodies with this section focusing specifically on our privates. Before I go any further, I have to talk about "private parts"…

The fact that we call our sex parts "private parts" gives insight into how we view sex. It's true that everybody has their own parts and that "no" means "no", but when we make a point to be secretive and private about talking sex, we as a society start having problems.

Actually, there are more and more people talking about private parts, but not as it relates to sex. People involved with homosexual activity are pushing for homosexual marriages and sex education from their perspective being taught to little kids, but they aren't going into much detail. They're leaving a lot of stuff "private", but I'm not.

If the agenda is to push homosexual, bisexual and transexual activity…don't be shy. Teach the little kids that homosexual activity between 2 dudes means one guy bends over and the other guy puts his dick in the bent-over guy's butt when they have sex.

Let the kids know that when 2 females involved in homosexual activity attempt to have sex…they can't because neither one of them has a dick. In order for them to have "sex", one of them has to pull out a fake dick, strap it on and then "hump" on her girlfriend without her fake dick ever ejaculating and let's not stop there…

Tell the kids that a person involved in the transexual lifestyle has done one of 3 things:

1.   **He** has gotten a risky surgery to get his dick and balls cut off and is taking female hormone pills to try and become a female. He also has undergone surgeries to have fake titties sewn on his chest in an attempt to look like a female, even though the purpose of titties isn't for show: they are to produce milk to feed and nourish newborn and young babies OR

2.   **She** has undergone a risky surgery to get her vagina closed up and had a fake dick and balls sewn on her body. She also has undergone another surgery to get her titties cut off to make her "chest" look more like a man's OR

3.   **He** still has his dick and balls but is taking female hormone pills to try and look feminine or **she** still has a uterus but is taking male hormone pills to try and grow a beard to look more masculine.

Do you see all of the confusion? Confusion is a typical result of not following God's laws for us in a certain area of our lives. In this case, the confusion is a result of not following God's laws and rules for good sex. God's design and purpose for our sex parts is simple: the man puts his dick inside the female's vagina. That's it and that's all, well, there's the aspect of a man and a woman having anal and oral sex, but the true basic design and function for the dick and va-jay-jay is to make babies and anal and oral sex ain't gonna get that done.

God's sex is extremely simple and erotic! The shame is a lot of people who claim to love God don't like to talk about sex or they act like you're not supposed to like it. Do you know why they call the sex position "Missionary Style"? I don't, but based on what I know about Christians and sex, I'm assuming it has something to do with female, Christian missionaries having sex with the man on top of the woman and aren't interested in getting bent over, doing 6-9's or Reverse Cowgirl. Anyways...

At the end section of every book, I have a couple of essays that are relevant to that particular book topic and they are called "Private Matter" essays. These are essays where I openly share my view on abortion, homosexual activity, alcohol, religion and other things people like to only talk about in private.

That being said, I want to share with you an essay about sex and Christians. I wrote it because I was frustrated with both sex and Christians. I was never formally taught about the pleasure and the actual act of sex from the church or my Christian education. I was frustrated because I like to use the words dick, coochie, ass and titties, but as a Christian, I was constantly being told not to use that type of language and that I was immoral and wicked. I couldn't even use the term doggie-style without being condemned by pastors, even though I have a dick, I like my wife's coochie, her ass and her titties and we like to have sex doggie-style.

Are we evil and immoral? Are we misusing marriage sex?

Are Christians supposed to act and talk like this? Isn't good, fun

sex a part of marriage? I thought so and I think so and I'm having

it. Check out this Private Matter Bonus Essay that talks bluntly

about Christianity and sex from my view and then we'll get back

into the rest of the book:

LOVE LANGUAGE OF CHRISTIANS

I am married and me and my wife love God and we love

sex. We like to fuck or make love. We don't like to have sexual

intercourse. Does that mean we don't love God? Since we

made sure we legalized our marriage in a church before God,

does using the word "fuck" mean we have disrespected our

sexual marriage vows to God? If we love God, does that mean

we are supposed to use King James talk when it comes to bedroom talk? I don't believe so.

How are Christians supposed to talk when it comes to sex and love? That is a question that should be debated and discussed in the church. But the church doesn't know how to talk about it…so I will.

Before I was married, I used to tell females, "Yes, I want you to suck my dick." I NEVER said, "Yes, I would like it if you put my penis in your mouth and receive oral sex from you." I NEVER just pulled my dick out and kind of smiled at her and looked from her mouth to my dick and back to her mouth hoping she would get the idea that I want my dick sucked. I openly said it then and now that I am married, I have to be just as open with her and vice versa.

If my wife just sat there with her legs open waiting for me to suck on her clit without a formal invitation…that shit ain't happenin'. She needs to feel free to express what she wants. I take that back. Actually, when you're married, there is a beautiful code you establish and nothing needs to be said. When I pull my dick out and lay back and smile at her, she knows what to do. When she lays with her legs open and raises her right eyebrow, I know what to do.

Now that I'm married, does that mean I can never say to my wife, "The kids are gone for the night, so you know we 'bout to get our fuck on all over the house. I want you to walk around naked so I can look at your sexxxy ass all day and when I can't take it anymore, I'm gonna grab you, turn you around, bend you over and fuck the shit out of you." Is that how married Christians are supposed to talk? Is that permissible Christian language?

Some of you may think I'm disgusting and that I am not a good Christian because I want to fuck my sexxxxy wife instead of wanting to "have sexual intercourse with my wife."

Some of you may think I'm disgusting and that I am not a good Christian because I want to lick my wife's pussy until she cums instead of wanting to "lick her in her clitoral/vaginal region until she reaches a climax."

Some of you may think I'm disgusting and that I am not a good Christian because I openly tell my wife to "turn around and put your ass in my face so I can kiss it. I think you have a sexxxy ass and I can't keep my mutha fuckin' lips and tongue off of that sexxxy thang" instead of openly telling my wife "Can you please turn around? I really like your buttocks and I would like it if you would bend over in front of me so I can kiss it. I just love the sight and feel of your rear end so much that I can't stop kissing all over it."

The point I am trying to make is that I don't believe you have to go all King James in the bedroom when you have sex as a Christian, married couple. God made sex to be enjoyable. One of the authors in the Bible said to the men, "get married to the woman you fall in love with as a youth and enjoy her breasts…" Another author in the Bible said, "the marriage bed is sacred and something for a husband and wife to enjoy however they see fit."

If that's really true, if my wife and I are used to talking a certain love language before we were married, we should feel free to talk in that same language as a married couple if that is the language that makes us comfortable, keeps our sex life strong and keeps us faithful to each other.

If I'm married and have sexual desires that I can't express to my wife, I am going to be inclined to hit the strip clubs and bars more frequently so I can come across a female who "understands" me and who I can enjoy having sex with. Since marriage is a thing that God supports and created as the power-base of society, we need to be talking about these things BEFORE marriage.

At the same time, there has to be boundaries and limits. Just because I may want to have anal sex with my wife does not mean she has to comply and take it every week in her ass. We still have to compromise. Maybe she takes it like that on Valentine's Day, President's Day and our anniversary or something. That's for you two to decide.

My point is that it's your marriage and your sex life. The point is, you two need to talk about sex or your marriage will fall the fuck apart. If you're a guy and secretly want to have sex with other guys, that's some shit your wife needs to know BEFORE you get married. We should all be at the point where we can share our views on sex and decide whether or not to move on together or get off the train.

Sex is an important element of marriage that needs to be talked about. When I look back at the people in my church when I was growing up, I can tell you that there was only one couple, and I won't say who it is, that looked like they were having sex. All the rest of the married couples looked like zombies. I never saw anybody sneak and hold hands or saw a couple share a laugh with another couple and the wife blush and kiss her husband on the cheek.

I went to an all-white church and that's what I saw. Anytime I went to white churches, that is the vibe I got. I have to go a step further and say I got the same vibe from all-black churches as well.

My experience with church and sex was that it never happened until…until somebody got a divorce because the wife was cheating or the husband had a full-blown porn addiction that was out of control. There was a pastor who committed suicide because he was hooked on phone sex and spending hundreds of dollars a month. He felt guilty and felt like he couldn't share that with anybody. Kirk Franklin, a famous gospel singer, came out and said he had a major porn addiction. He had porn videos stashed all around the house behind every television or something crazy like that. It happens. It happens to anybody and it needs to be talked about. It's major incidents like that when you realized people in the church had sex problems or were actually having sex.

I have to add this to be fair, Joel Osteen has a wife who looks like she wants to have fun sexually, she's attractive and dresses in a modern, conservative-yet-sexxxy style. That's refreshing to see. Her husband Joel on the other hand, with his perfectly set and sprayed hair style, bleached white teeth with that permanent smile on his face and that joyful message he delivers every Sunday, looks like he could care less whether they had sex or not. I mean, they do have a couple of kids as proof, but other than that...you can tell Joe ain't really hittin' that like he's supposed to.

There is a twist to all of this. When I was in church, it was also the place where I saw plenty of sexxxxy females. An older friend of mine used to tell me that church was the best place to find a nice female. I think he must have been talking to a lot of church-going females as well because the single ladies in church had a tendency to dress sexxxy; unlike the married females who tended to want to leave the impression that they were sanctified, highly favored, blessed and content to be married.

It's unreal for us to think a pastor doesn't get turned on by females outside of his wife. If he didn't, that means he is either into homosexual activity (and should not be in the pulpit) or he is in complete denial of his maleness.

I've asked a couple preachers about this and even though they were married, they still say they see women as being attractive and even sexxxy. They even admitted to me that they still look at a sexxxy female walking by sometimes. For them though, they say the difference is their thought process: just because they are married doesn't mean they don't see or recognize female beauty...it just means they understand how serious marriage is and straying from his wife for some sex is not worth falling out of favor with God, destroying a marriage, destroying the power-base of the family structure, causing emotional harm to the kids and a bunch of other chaos that results from lacking sexual discipline.

If you think I'm being unrealistic, feel free to look around your church and see how many couples look like they are having fun sexually. Look at your pastor and his wife and see if you think he is hittin' it from the back and they are enjoying doing the reverse-cowgirl position or doing 69's.

When I look around congregations, I see plenty of sexxxy women I would like to have sex with (this of course is before I was married). What I don't see is married couples looking sexually satisfied; especially the pastor. Nine out of ten times the pastor's wife has a dress that drags down to her ankles and a shirt that's long-sleeved and buttoned all the way to the top button...looking like she walked straight off the television show

Bonanza, Little House on the Prairie or some other old-school show.

Do I want my pastor's wife wearing short, sexxxy skirts with high heels and a short top so her ass shows? No. I'm not saying that. What I am saying is that when a person is having fun sexually, it shows in the way they walk, talk and dress and it would be nice to see a pastor-wife team looking like they are human and like they like sex.

In the end, I think, as one who was sexually irresponsible and a Christian for many years, that it's important that the church grow some balls and takes a stand on sexuality. Everybody else openly pushes their thoughts and agenda for sex.

People involved with homosexual activity have openly let it be known that they want to teach public school kids at early ages that homosexual activity is cool and it's something that has no negative or confusing impact on the family and society. Not cool. Very confusing.

The media has been pushing shows that send us the message that it's okay if you're a man and you feel like a woman...just cut your dick off, get a fake vagina, get some big, fake-ass titties sown onto your chest and BAM! YOU ARE NOW A LADY!!! Not.

It's time for somebody to stand up and start talking about the beauty of waiting to have sex until marriage.

It's time for somebody to stand up and start talking about how they did have sexual desires that went against the Bible and God, but they took the time to fight those feelings and not just fall victim to any and every sexual desire and urge that came their way.

It's time for somebody to stand up and start talking about the fact that getting fake titties doesn't make you a female any more than getting a fake dick sewn on your body makes you a man.

Whatever your view is it's important because it's your view. We may not all agree, but what we can agree on is the results. Start looking at the results of certain sexual behavior and see if it's a good thing or a bad thing. Doing this, I believe, will allow the natural design and order of sex to continue to be a beautiful thing.

It all starts with 1) your view on sex, 2) talking about sex and 3) making sex education an important topic in church, the home and schools.

How was it? I know I wouldn't have to ask any of you who are a part of the Dutch, Christian Reformed Church and over the age of 65 "how was it?" because I know you most likely haven't even gotten this far and if you did, it was by accident. For those of you still reading, stay focused 'cause there's more where that came from and it's coming up next...

Let's jump right into it and, just so you know, my perspective is based on what I have learned and experienced from applying God's laws to my life as best as possible. I'm going to run down what I think our private parts are for based on God's instructions and examples and I think you will be shocked at how simple and sexxxy this shit is:

1.   **God created planet Earth and designed and planned on having humans manage it.** You cannot deny the design, laws and planning all around you. Since you cannot deny that, you cannot deny there is a designer behind it. *You* can deny the existence of God and as God being the designer/creator, but I can't. As you have read from the earlier chapters in this book, God designed humans to be the top-dogs on the planet. Our brains and bodies are designed on a higher level than any of our nearest species competitors. The part I'm focusing on in this

chapter is our private parts. God only created 2 humans. He created a man and a woman. According to His plan and design, that's all He had to make. Why? That's all He had to make because He instructed that 1st human couple, Adam and Eve, to fill the Earth with humans so that humans could continue to manage the Earth and control all other life on it. Why didn't God make a bunch of humans? He should have because it takes billions of humans to manage the Earth properly. He made Adam with a dick and Eve with a uterus...that's why! The purpose of a man and woman getting together as a couple is to have sex and create more humans!

2.   **The male human in marriage.** God made males with a dick. He told them what to do with it. All throughout the Bible we learn that God wanted the man to use his dick to make his wife happy and to have babies. Don't believe me? In the book of Genesis 1 verse 22 is where he instructed the man to use his dick to make babies and in Deuteronomy 24 verse 5 God says, "...if a man has recently married, he must not be sent to war or

have any other duty placed on him. For 1 year he is to be free to stay at home and bring happiness to his wife…" See? God wants us to be free to enjoy sex and marriage so much so, that He wants anybody who gets married to be able to at least have one good year of focusing on each other and making each other happy…and that includes sex! Let's talk about sex outside of marriage for a second. If you have sex outside of marriage, this act of a man spending time alone with his wife making her happy will be hard to do for several reasons. For me, I could give you 7 reasons off the top of my head: I had 7 kids before I got married. How am I supposed to be able to focus on just Netta for a year? Am I supposed to ignore my previous kids? Did you see how I said "my previous kids?" I said that because I wasn't the only one who had sex before marriage. Netta came to the marriage with 2 boys from a previous relationship and they lived with us. Trust me, during the 1st year, and even now, we have tried our best to "take care of each other" but it is *extremely* hard with 2 active boys under the age of 6 living under the same roof as you. I'm sure some of you parents reading this book know exactly what I'm

talking about. You see, if we had both followed God's laws for sex

and gotten married 1st and had sex afterwards, it would have

been easy for the husband to please his wife for the 1st year; but

there's the flipside: if she had married her kid's father and I had

married one of my kid's mothers (I have kids by 6 different

women), we would not have gotten married. Can you see all of

the confusion and twists and turns that could have kept marriage

simple and sexually satisfying from the start? The good news is,

from my experience, I got personal with God and asked Him to

help me get things back to normal and He did. My wife and I

didn't work the entire 1st year we were married. We weren't lazy,

but I felt God leading us to be able to have time to get to know

each other, bond, solidify our friendship and our walk with God

and then step out into the world and take care of His business. So

far, it has worked, but it always wasn't an easy thing. You know

what? I almost drifted off to a topic that one of my other books,

"Tongue Ink: Part One" covered, so let me stay on track and focus on this book and on the man's dick and the woman's uterus...

3.   **Anatomy of a dick.** To keep shit simple, the man has a dick and 2 balls. That's the way God made it with the goal to keep putting your dick in and out a vagina until you release, climax, cum, ejaculate, orgasm or whatever else you wanna call it. The act of releasing releases the seed in a man's balls and that seed goes into the female's vagina and travels to the uterus and that's basically how you make babies. Do you know what gives a man the most pleasure with his dick? It's when he's pushing and pulling it inside a hole until he cums. That's where we have problems in our personal lives and in society. Men think their dick is for their pleasure, so, without any accountability to God, they feel free to shove their dick in any hole on any person, animal or plastic doll. It is true that the best pleasure a man gets is from working his dick in and out a hole, but there needs to be rules. There are rules for every, single act on this planet from driving to the natural laws of gravity...so why not the dick? Here's what God

has to say about it: the dick is designed to get pleasure from going in and out a hole BUT the hole has to be attached to a female with the most purposeful and productive hole being the vagina. Simple, isn't it? The male dick is designed to give the man, and hopefully his female mate, pleasure and the main law to achieve maximum pleasure is it has to be put into a female's hole. Ejaculating is the endgame for vaginal sex and "decorating the cake" is the end game for oral sex. Climaxing and cumming in the vagina are such an important and essential "task" for humanity, God made that the absolute most bestest feeling one can ever hope to achieve on this planet! I know! I chased that high with cocaine for years and never got there. To take this one step further, the "most purposeful and productive" female hole is the vagina, the vagina is designed to naturally lubricate itself. I mean, technically the mouth is too, but getting some head/oral sex doesn't have the productive aspect of producing life that the vagina has.

That's a wrap for my basic points, biology and anatomy of our "private parts". Actually, I wanted to get into the female "private parts", but as a man, I think it's best I leave that to the professionals and by that, I mean any female.

Let's stop being so private about our private parts.

Let's start teaching kids at a young age the beauty of sex. Shit! It's how they got here, isn't it?

Let's talk to our children about porn.

Let's share with our kids our experiences and sex. Some of us started at an early age. Share your experience with some kid who is a teen parent.

Talk about abortion. And I'm talking all the real, shameful, painful aspects of it and how to avoid it.

Talk about the realities of transexual and homosexual activity. Kids are being shown in movies and commercials that it's cool, so they're getting involved in it without fully realizing the

surgical dangers (transexual activity) and the inability to use their

bodies to achieve maximum, sexual pleasure (homosexual

activity).

Let's not just share with the younger generation: let's

share with each other as grown ass adults about our private parts.

If you need help getting the conversation started…grab some

extra copies of this book and have the people you want to talk to

read this 1st. Just a thought…

I did so much preaching, teaching and sharing while I was caring in the main sections of this book that I don't wanna repeat myself in the form of more preaching, teaching and sharing while I'm caring…so I won't. You know my view on God, our bodies and our responsibility, so now I just want you to check out my views in these short essays on a couple of topics that are related to this book. Here they are:

FATHER TIME

Contrary to popular opinion, when God asked the question, "Would a mere mortal, a man, rob God?" I think it had less to do with money and more to do with time. Pastors love to quote this verse in attempts to make the congregation feel guilt. It's as though the pastor is like, "Hey! You better pay attention and stop

stealing from God! God doesn't like it when you don't tithe, in fact,

He makes it clear you are supposed to give the full amount of your

tithe! So, stop stealing from God and dig as deep as your ass can in

them pockets and put it in the plate! Thief!"

That passage about stealing from God comes from Malachi

3. God does say we are robbing Him when we don't bring our tithe

BUT if you look at Malachi 1, you find the real reason behind tithing

that interests Him…

In Malachi 1 God says, "A son honors his father, and a slave

honors his master. If I am a father, where is the honor due me? If

I am a master, where is the respect due me?"

In my view, when God says, "…where is the honor and

respect due me?" He is considering THAT robbery. NOT giving

God the honor and respect that you owe Him is stealing from Him.

When you don't tithe, you aren't respecting or honoring His laws

and when you don't respect someone's laws that means you don't respect them. And when you don't respect them, you are basically stealing from them. You are not giving them what you owe them.

Money is simply a tool to measure time. You work or invest your time and experiences that you've gathered over your life, and you receive money in return. Money is only a physical rendering of time. Money takes time from being something you can't see, to something you can physically see and measure.

When you give money in the collection plate, you are giving time. If you have a lot of money, that means a lot of people have invested their time and purchased something from you with money. In essence, you are now responsible for their time. You are a time-manager. What are you going to do with all the time you have?

Are you going to take all of their time and buy yourself a new yacht each year? Are you going to use their time to buy drugs and get drunk? Are you going to use that time to make sure you and your family alone are taken care of?

We are managers of this Earth. When we give tithe, in my view, it is symbolically acknowledging God's system of management He trusted us with and that is giving God the honor and respect He is due.

So, are we supposed to bring money to the church? Yes. But it's the symbolism behind the money...not the currency value of it.

I think it's time pastors started learning about the principles behind the actions necessary to represent the kingdom of Heaven...and that's my view.

The porn industry is a home-wrecker/relationship killer.

The porn industry is a career-killer. The porn industry is

manhood-killer. How do I know? Because I used to love porn and

everything attached to it: sexual fantasy life, sex drugs, sex,

drugs...

From reading the different stories in the Bible you can see

how sex and lust affected many people's lives negatively...just like

it does today. It made King David, a great Man of God, commit 1st

degree murder. A King was willing to give up half of his kingdom

for a lap dance. These may be situations that occurred a long

time ago, but I am sure we all know, or are that person, who has

made some dumb decisions because we allowed sex and lust to

be the deciding factors.

The porn industry is an industry that faithfully reaps in several billion dollars a year with no signs of slowing down. IF YOU DO NOT GET A HANDLE ON YOUR SEXUAL DESIRES AND EXPECTATIONS, THIS INDUSTRY WILL CONTINUE TO TEAR UP HOME LIVES AND KILL DREAMS.

Sex sells. I have seen commercials for cookies that show a sexxxy female dancing around with some tight, fitting jeans on and some cleavage showing talking about how much she loves milk and cookies. I am lactose intolerant and I almost went out to buy some milk and cookies because they made it seem like if I presented a snack of milk and cookies to a female that she would somehow, in anticipation of me bringing here this snack, be waiting around in some sexxxy jeans or a nice short skirt, eagerly awaiting my phone call letting her know I was on the way with her favorite: milk and cookies.

Lucky for you, we are about to pull back the curtain and see how this industry can, and needs to be, brought to its knees.

As a man, I can only give it to you from a man's point of view; and to be more specific I can only share my point of view. And to keep things simple, I will use the term "porn-activity" to refer to watching pornos, strippers and dabbling with escorts/prostitutes interchangeably. Here's how it got me:

Home Wrecker/Relationship Killer – Porn activity females are not portraying their nurturing, wifely, motherly sides. They show every side *except* those sides. This all appears harmless enough, but the more you watch and get involved, the more you begin to view women as simply sex objects. And why not??? They appear to be so happy and willing and as a man, you naturally want to make a female happy.

1.   The more accustomed to fantasy women, the less I was able to deal with a real woman. I was able to have all my

basic female needs taken care of without all the talking and commitment.

2.   Women I talked to said they would never consider marriage to a man who was involved in porn-activity because they know they can't compete with a female in that industry.

3.   I got addicted to cocaine. Drugs and alcohol put you in a state of temporary "happiness". Cocaine kept my fantasy sex life alive; while killing any hopes of having a real sex life.

4.   The more my failures at having a real relationship grew because of my drug addiction and shame, the more my attempts to get in relationships did long-lasting damage to my girlfriends and the children that were the result of these relationships.

Career Killer – Having a career for me was out of the question. For each person this may be different. I allowed porn-activity to kill my career dreams and goals because of my inability to deal with real life.

1.	I longed to be in a relationship so bad that I got high to enjoy my fantasy relationship any chance I could. Having a career and a drug addiction don't mix.

2.	It became harder and harder for me to see myself in a real career achieving real results when I had no confidence in my dealings with reality.

3.	It's hard to realize your dreams of being a big-time business owner and investor when you spend your savings on porn-related activities.

Manhood Killer – Becoming a man, like anything else in life, is the results of your habits. My habits were stripping me of my confidence and manhood with each bad decision.

1.	A man respects a woman. The porn industry teaches men to treat women with disrespect, wanting them only as sex objects.

2.	A man knows how to handle reality. The porn industry teaches men to sacrifice reality for fantasy.

3.   A man knows how to budget his finances.

Budgeting money for sexual fantasies is not practical or wise.

4.   A man loves commitment. The porn industry

wants men to constantly be on the lookout for new and exciting

sexual experiences.

There is a point in your life where it becomes harder to go

back to the way it was. Kind of like a cucumber: once it becomes

a pickle...it can't be a cucumber anymore. Your life is the sum

results of habits. Someone acted towards you based on the

habits they were taught or you acted the way you did based on

your habits.

The Bible teaches us and shows us and warns us about sex.

There are plenty of examples that show the goods and the bads.

Sex was designed to be a beautiful act that compliments the natural

attraction between a man and a woman to create children. We wouldn't be here without it. Our ability to enjoy life depends on our ability to enjoy sex the way it was meant to be. The BIBLE: Basic Instructions Before Leaving Earth...about sex. That's my new view and I'm stickin' to it.

SPERM: The Ultimate Seed

Sperm is the ultimate seed because of its power and ability to create humans.

1.   Everything on this planet and in this universe was made for humans.

- The ground and water provide natural nutrition for plants.

- Through the process of photosynthesis, plants make the air breathable for humans and through consumption provide the human body with every necessary nutrient it needs.

- Every human cell in our body needs water and without it, a human would typically die within 3-4 days. The chemical make-up of water, H20, makes water the only natural liquid that the human body needs to replenish itself and survive.

- If the Earth was closer or farther away from the Sun...we would all die and if the Earth was to move faster or slower...we would all die.

2. Humans are the most powerful life force on this planet.

- No other life form can control its environment like humans.

- Nothing that is unnatural would have existed without humans: cars, boats, bridges, computers, etc.

- No other life form has the ability to manipulate every element on this planet to its will

3. On the spiritual side of things:

- No other life form has a spiritual level comparable to humans

- No other life form has the ability to control its spiritual destiny

- Humans are the image of God

A man's body is the only life-form that produces semen, the seed of humanity. The following are some of the activities that are designed to weaken a man by stripping him of the proper use of his seed:

1.   Lust

• Masturbating/jacking is a waste of seed/power

2.   Contraceptives/Safe sex

• They are counterproductive to married couples because responsible, natural fatherhood truest form of natural power for a man

• They kill the potential of the seed/life

3.   Abortion

• Destroys the female's body

• Kills the most powerful life form that exists

Seeds are important. Jesus said "If you have faith the size of a mustard seed you can move mountains." When God created the Earth, He told man "I give you every seed-bearing fruit for you and the animals to eat." Every natural, living thing comes from a seed.

<u>For men</u>: You have power. Learn the correct way to plant your seed.

<u>For women</u>: You have power. Learn the correct way to select your seed.

<u>For parents</u>: You have power. Learn the correct way to nourish your seed.

HOMOSEXUAL ACTIVITY

I am against homosexual activity. Not because I don't like it. Not because I think it's weird. Not because I don't understand it...I am against homosexual activity because it goes against God's laws.

To be clear and fair, homosexual activity is only one of God's laws regarding sex that I am against. This may sound hypocritical, and people who are involved in homosexual activity or people who are against God, love to say that, but yes, I used to break all kinds of God's laws on sex.

God said we aren't supposed to cheat on our husbands or wives...I slept with a couple of married women in my day. That was wrong only because it went against God's laws and I had to stop. Did I want to stop? Not really, but I had no choice: it was either follow God's laws or my own laws.

God said we aren't supposed to lust. That means we aren't supposed to allow ourselves to see someone and view them as a piece of meat. I used to deal with that when I had a major porn addiction.

I would get high and watch porn for hours until my eyeballs dried up. I loved it. The rush of the endorphin releasing drug with the rush of the porn-visual had me hooked for years. I had to stop doing it. Did I want to stop? Not really, but I had no choice: it was either follow God's laws or my own laws.

People, particularly in the church, who love to point out the wrongs of homosexual activity, tend to forget about God's other laws surrounding sex. They like to point out homosexual activity while they themselves are lusting at strip clubs, hooked on porn or phone sex, cheating on their husband or wife or having sex with a very, very close family member.

This topic has been beaten up a lot and blown out of proportion. At this stage in the game, I understand 99% of humans are not involved in homosexual activity and 99% of humans don't understand homosexual activity and 99% of humans are scared to speak up and state their view because of media, personal, professional and social backlash.

I am not concerned with any of that, so I can speak freely. I follow God's laws as best as I can and I know He designed this place and that He runs shit, to if anybody has a problem with me stating my views…oh well. Get over it because I'm not stating my views, I'm stating God's views.

Anything I've done in the past that went against God's laws is something I have both an obligation to stop doing, openly confess what it is I was doing AND help people who are interested in following God's laws to stop as well. While we're on the homosexual subject, let's also be clear:

1.   There is no such thing as homophobia or homophobic. People aren't scared of people who are involved in homosexual activity. That's a very effective term that people

involved in homosexual activity have used to get their "opponents" to shut the fuck up, back down and let homosexual activity become a normal thing in society.

2.	I don't call people involved in homosexual "homosexuals, gay, questioning, queer, bi-sexual, lesbian, stud, dike, fish, top or bottom" or whatever other labels are out there. I refuse to characterize someone by their sexual choices and preferences. If you like homosexual activity, you are simply a man or woman who likes homosexual activity.

3.	I am not changing my basic understanding of the English language and start calling people "him/her/she/he." That's about the stupidest, dumbest thing I could ever do. It's not that I don't respect everyone's freedom of choice...it's simply because I know how to speak English and I know that "he" is a pronoun that describes a single, individual male. There is enough changing of the English language with words like "bad", "shit" and "lit" meaning a thousand different things. I sure as fuck am not about to start calling "him" a "her" and "she" a "he" or "me" a "him/her/he/she."

4.	Any State or country can legalize homosexual marriage, and any human who follows God's laws can *not* give a shit. I guess if a State says humans can marry animals that I, as a business owner, would have to start allowing spousal support for a German Shepherd's husband or wife that is an employee of mine? Get the fuck out of here. Won't happen. I operate along God's laws and am under His government's protection, guidance and care, so make whatever laws you want: if they go directly against God's laws, I will never follow them and you will never force me to.

In the end, do whatever *you* want. Suck on whoever *you* want. Fuck whoever *you* want. Marry whoever *you* want. Use fake dicks when *you* have fake sex if *you* want. Buy a fake vagina and have fake titties if *you* want...do whatever *you* want if *you* want to follow *your* own rules.

When you want to wake up like I had to do and start following God's nice and easy rules for sex...let me know. I had to learn the hard way, but I might be able to help you switch over…if

that's what *you* want.

Personal Development Notes

Personal Development Notes

Personal Development Notes